After the First World

After the First World

CHRISTINE CASSON

After the First World

Copyright © 2008
by Christine Casson

cover design by Trish Hadley

Published by

~ STAR CLOUD PRESS® ~

6137 East Mescal Street
Scottsdale, Arizona 85254-5418

ISBN:

978-1-932842-25-8 — $14.95

Library of Congress Control Number: 2008920149

Printed in the United States of America

Acknowledgments

Many thanks to the editors of the following journals and anthologies where these poems have appeared:

Agenda: "Villanelle for My Father, Drifting," "My Father's Hands"
Alabama Literary Review: "Impromptu," "Apophatic," "Slip Knot,"
     "Arrangement"
Dalhousie Review: "The Beach at Hull"
DoubleTake: "The Portion"
Natural Bridge: "Exile," "Learning Death"
Slant: "Guide"
South Dakota Review: "Interlude: Jones Beach"

"To Melville, Near Death" appears in *Fashioned Pleasures*
(Parallel Press, 2005).

"To the South" appears in *Never Before: Poems About First Experiences*
(Four Way Books, 2005).

"We All Knock" appears in *Conversation Pieces: Poems That Talk to Other Poems* (Everyman's Library, 2007).

Cover Art: Jacob Vosmaer (Dutch, 1584-1641), A Vase with Flowers, ca. 1618. Oil on wood; 33-1/2 x 24 5/8 in. (85.1x62.5 cm)
The Metropolitan Museum of Art, Purchase, 1871 (71.5)
Photograph © 1993 The Metropolitan Museum of Art

for
Lawrence V. Casson
and
for Daniel Tobin

Contents

III. AS IF OF WINGS

This World is not Conclusion
A species stands beyond—
Invisible as Music—

... the Garden in the Brain
This Curiosity

—Emily Dickinson

I. Learning the River

IMPROMPTU

—She sang beyond the genius of the sea.

She stands there, ironing. Her arm moves forth
and back—her body slightly bent—with each
drag across the board and then a pause . . .

She shifts the shirt's yoke, adjusts its angle
on the arm; water sputters into steam;
her hand draws slow until the wrinkles

disappear. She's staked her claim in the living room.
She likes to move her work around the house—
the sewing she can do most anywhere.

Bored, she puts a record on; extending chords,
a piano's hammered keys, consort
with the vapor's hiss, then veer and fall.

She rests her iron on its heel, recalls
her own impulse to sing, to feel the tones
vibrating in her throat, the firm funnel

of her chest supporting air, and soon
the letting go, each note freed to settle
in the world along with ordinary sounds.

She listens to the cello's quick response,
the cadence and diminishment of strings
that rise above the pressure and release

of rosined bow. Its slurred ascent wakes
her need to sing. She draws in breath, and more,
resists the tautness of her sluggish lungs,

her torso become an amphora of air,
pliant, to control the stream of breath
that burgeons, lifting from her throat

to fill the room. The fullness of her chest
is more than this. The late-day sun persists
through half–drawn shades, reddening, it burnishes

the walls, drifts in lustred mullions on the floor,
like the portioning of breath that resonates,
augments and falls, flares on the discarded shirt.

MIMOSA

Late May and its blossoms would burst
into flames, effusion of color, innumerable
flower after flower, all through summer
into early fall. *A Mimosa tree*, said my mother,
disapproving of our neighbor's choice.
What a mess they make,
month after month, and those seed pods
rotting on the ground.
My father would sweep and sweep
the walk, hard, to remove those fallen
blooms until not one remained, that in summer heat
would fasten to the pavement,
overripe, leaving rosy stains.
I couldn't see their harm.
No ordinary leaves, but ferns fanning the air,
falling from smooth limbs
like lace robes; each flower a mass
of silk threads, hot pink
lightening to pink-white at its base, feathers
bunched into ball-like clusters,
to adorn a movie star's slipper
or sew into a long plumed scarf,
one I'd wear with those forbidden high heels
tucked far back in my mother's closet, wrapped and stuffed
with tissue, saved for that rare occasion
when only dress-up clothes would do,

carefully removed from their box
and placed on my small feet.
Or I'd gather seedpods, dry like old paper,
bend them open to reveal brown beads inside,
arrange them on the ground
strand after strand into a gypsy's necklace
until the wind would scatter my design.
Evenings, its leaflets would fold inward,
like a shy gathering of flirtatious skirts
to cooler green within-ness,
the woman who, after a day of offering up,
returns, quiet, to her room.

My Father's Hands

They come to me now that they've been stilled,
long shapely fingers, the white crescent edge
of each nail, a spray of dark hair—
She'd speak of them often, my mother,
who would read hands like a palmist,
the dorsal side, character revealed in their length,
shape, whether bony or full: this offspring of the fin,
how in everyone's the veins throb with blood.

My father's danced across the harmonica
retrieved from shallows of his dresser drawer,
his fingers like eighth notes on a vocal score—
or poised above the movement of a watch.
He'd tease into place a bracelet's recalcitrant links,
coax a paintbrush to surety of line,
or smooth my hair in awkward affection—
long minutes so rare I wouldn't move.

His hands float on memory's undercurrents—
five jointed tributaries on carpal bones,
still reptilian. I want to crawl toward sea,
prints gripping sand, each whorled impress
wind-sifted, awash, wade through pools
of my own palms into deep, until, submerged,
I learn again to breathe the watery air
where tides gather in the ocean's sweep.

CHRISTINE CASSON

GUIDE

As we rushed to catch the plane to carry us home,
away from this brief life overseas
where Dublin traffic jams under Georgian facades;
as I shoved belongings into suitcase and box,
cab humming to return—
tucked what I could into this crevice or that,
fought zippers, clasps; still, I was forced
to leave effects behind—
I, who would collect the past in things,
not trusting memory's hold—
like those photos of my childhood house,
the rooms dressed, then bare before the move,
as if meaning were exposed
in the camera's click. And that single prayer card
I saved to keep my dead father near,
its doe-eyed Christ carrying one of his many lambs,
rendered in cool pastels,
the image I'd seen time and time before,
tucked inside pocket or purse,
slipped into that travel guide I knew I'd keep,
chronicle of where we'd been.
How could I know what I would or wouldn't miss
in that rush to the street below,
our patient driver working every space,
engine thrumming—*hurry no time*—
what's unneeded left behind, and mess,
and garbage shoved in bags to haul away?

The mind will discriminate, choose this or that:
lover, work, perhaps a favored child—
but how can it know the consequences of its choice?
I ask that question now, back in these suburbs
of endless tract homes like a mirror image
turned upon itself—
the nervous laughter, a surprised screech,
some dog's purposeless growl,
entrance into this carnival maze
of whining tools and gadgets—
Can we rest? How can we ever rest?
Another board to saw. Did you edge the lawn?—
where useless things abound, and more to buy,
even on TV: *we have everything you need,*
hand-vacs, knives, music for love and soul,
and girls, if you like, late at night—even girls—
and they're only eighteen—
And the silence, when it falls?
A moth dropping from a screen. And the prayer card lost
in my thoughtless rush,
that guidebook tossed away, then gathered
with the trash by indifferent hands—
what's gone as heavy as what remains.
Why can't we stand the sweet, simple present unadorned?

7   CHRISTINE CASSON

EXILE

Tall lights that blaze all night,
candescent glass, streets steaming shadow
into every crevice, and in the day,
air lustered with dust and grime . . .
Drawn to broken pavement, alleyways,
I never left that city's steel shimmer.
From far away, I imagine bridges,
vaulted roofs, plunge to depths
to shuttle under roads at speeds
near unbearable; emerge through miles into air
that thrums with noise so electric
it raises hair on my arms and neck.

I've made a garden where I am,
a sanctuary so profuse
as to almost fool the traveler,
who needs to root and thrive, briefly,
before moving on. Adjacent to the fence
a hole waits, and a trellis
this new clematis will wind itself around.
It will twist leaves and stem
to the sturdy grille, wrought-iron fronds
lifting rod-like from the soil,
imagined by some worker at a desk

shuffling patterns of stylized foliage,
pale in the fluorescent glare
of *Golden Pond Garden Forms*,
who dreams himself outdoors
soaked by rain or sweating in the sun—
and these celosia flaring towards the sky.

CHRISTINE CASSON

MAKING DO

Each day after school, if the weather holds,
you come outside to play alone, hopping
the broken bricks and stones behind your house.

You must be six or seven. The yard, half toys,
half junk, looks dangerous: a rusted ladder,
rotting planks and two by fours, remnants

of a shed with nails, a pickup's flattened tires,
that rusting wheelchair parked in last year's leaves,
and an outsized doghouse for all your toys.

Some days you drive your plastic truck through all
these horded obstacles, legs pumping hard
as you steer your way along the path you've made,

or you patiently sit on your see-saw,
as if someone might come to sit across,
lift you high enough to see beyond the fence.

When you swing your orange bat with such intent,
I can almost see the ball fly, hear the cheers
as you run around the bases into home.

Today, you pretend to build. You strike
and strike again those gray decaying boards,
the metal hammer you rescued from the dirt
sounding out your work, your making do.

SCREENSAVER

On mine the towers flick by, image
after image, two square rods
set on their heels, higher
than the Apollo rockets
as if, without liftoff,
they could reach the moon,
as if some child had balanced
block on top of block
to see how high
they might be piled
before they fell. They show up
in almost every view,
like that relative in every photo.
In those suburbs where I grew up,
houses, lawns that configure
my past, that flattened prospect—
I was drawn by skyscrapers,
crowds, the center of things,
to the elevated train
that would kneel, tuck
into the tunnel that ran
beneath the East River's arm,
the Island in its crook.

My brother built model rockets.
The kit arrived through the mail—

CHRISTINE CASSON

squares of balsa wood, a pattern,
paints, the blunt nosecone.
He and my father would draw and cut
each fin to size, sand and buff
the wood to a high sheen,
then paint, assemble the body—
the engine of rolled paper
and solid fuel propellant,
a hair-thin wire to carry
electric current from the launch pad,
engage the spark that would ignite
this missile into air, guided
by a narrow rod to ensure
its mission straight up into space.
They'd launch it at the park—
long stretches of bare field,
trees in the distance, a big sky.
After the countdown,
it surged upward to held
breaths, our fingers crossed
that it wouldn't fly so far as to be lost;
watched for the parachute
that would soften its descent.
Either way, it would float
or crash to earth, its fuel spent.

For seven years the city labored
on those towers, the outer wall
erected floor by floor
one hundred ten times over,
the work of Sisyphus
accomplished, its steel embrasures
launched so we could stand
on its observation deck,
camera in tow, tripods
for timed exposures,
my father and I fiddling
with apertures and film speeds,
confronted by a new depth of field.
Patiently, he spoke
of the intensity of light,
the picture's frame, taught me
to align those splintered images
to wholeness in the rangefinder.
I'd focus long and hard
on those crosscut streets below,
imagining how they would look
to its shuttered eye
and what it might miss,
what color or reflection lost
in the air's refractive grain,

CHRISTINE CASSON

the heights beneath us dwarfed
like the past receding
to a dense, shadowed grid
bridging into harbor,
the glittering beach,
the distant emulsion of haze.

Interlude: Jones Beach

If you drive to this crescent strand where tides rise quickly,
their greedy fingers reaching and mothers calling,
pulling toddlers to safety, surfers straining to stand—
if you see sand, miles of it like fine wheat dotted
with broken shells washed ashore, rented umbrellas
budding red and blue beneath seagulls that hover, sink
to scavenge at water's edge, wings flicking, or dance
an awkward two-step to the ocean's foaming pulse—
and if you stay into the evening when the moon rises
over the now empty beach bathed in liquid glass, glinting,
where music seeps from a far off boardwalk pavilion
and a middle-aged couple dance together, his hand
pressed to the small of her back, her head upturned, arm draped
lightly on his neck, their steps synchronous and sure—
then you'll know why, for so long, I've kept this chipped conch,
concentric curves, pearlescent, that listen, remember
against the undertow, its unbroken rush and stream.

Christine Casson

AUTUMN WATCH

A crow perches on a lamppost above the street,
balances on one foot, then the other,
extends its wings, draws them in again
as if in thought, as if to oversee
the season's machinations.
Licked by the sun's long tongue,
the tossed air plucks from stems
the leathered basil leaves,
the last tomatoes hung like bulbs
on lackluster vines the faded green
of old paint, barely able to hold
the weight of fruit that bends low,
rattles the table where a woman reads,
isolated bursts like the hand of a lover
ignored too long, or a needy child.

It growls its deep warning. Wrappers,
crumpled leaves, skitter through yards
as a couple make dinner, argue,
the slam of pots and utensils rising.
Their food begins to burn.
Down the block sauce simmers
in large pots. Aromas steep the air,
settle in the restaurant's bar that starts to fill,
women and men just come from work who laugh

when the bartender tells a racial joke—the one
about the parrot and the black man—
and no one willing to object. The wind sounds
like a cornered dog. The sun
purples the crow's descending sweep
and cicadas, warmed, ply their last songs.

CHRISTINE CASSON

VILLANELLE FOR MY FATHER, DRIFTING

My shovel works in whispered increments.
Its push and lift seem hardly to affect
this depth of snow, its smothering intent.

I've worked for hours, yet there's evidence
I'm getting nowhere. One would expect
some glimpse of road in steady increments,

some indication that energy hard spent
at burdened tasks might somehow resurrect
such labors from the weight of mere intent.

Instead this snow persists, impudent
as your illness that insistently detracts
from movement, stills your limbs in increments

and steals your speech. How could you circumvent
its steady course—words severed from their objects—
like these broad drifts obscuring my intent,

when all your life you took care to prevent
your falling ill? Your blurted words reflect
the burden of such weight, hushed increments
of loss increasing, and this sky's white intent.

LEARNING DEATH

Another morning's mouth yawns wide as a cat's.
I break eggs into a bowl. Each white clings
to its shell. Nothing entices. It all just sits,
like me. The gleam's gone out of the silver,
wood floors hooded with dust. Books lie,
mute stones on tabletops and shelves.
Breakfast done, I wash my plate: my thumbnail
scrapes the hardened yolk.

                    You bring red roses,
and as the days pass each opens in concert
with the rest, a perfect choreography of petals.
My father, these last months, unable to rise and walk,
crawled through the house, hands and knees icy
from bare floors. At twelve, my niece's underwear
are brightly stained. She scrubs them hard
to whiten them. Her mother, face flushed, fiftyish,
stands near an open window, flaps her skirts.

Your mother will not eat: she sits with head
to knees or goes to bed to lie, unmoving,
until dark. The Irish call it *ag foghlaim
an Glais*—learning the river—tell stories
of those who'd walk to hospital Christmas Eve,

demand to be alone, then face the wall to die.
As he lay chill and weighty on the sheets,
I watched my father skip one painful breath,
and in the next, master that lesson.

WOOD

-for Lotte-

Everything takes so long now you complain,
then talk about your friends I met last year:
gathered at your home for cake and tea served
on flowered china plates, each struggled
to walk or hear or see—repeated trips
to doctors and concern for children grown.

One has moved—too fragile to keep house,
she's living where she never thought she'd be—
a suite of disinfected rooms and halls—
and you less self-reliant than before
with your dull cane, hospital steel and gray,
grim support now your husband's gone.

When we speak you can hardly hold the words
after so much time alone. They rush from you
like seeds of drying chervil, wind-scattered,
planted in your garden years before,
your voice strong as the herb's tensile wisps
bordering your vegetables' furrowed beds,

CHRISTINE CASSON

the work of careful mornings on your knees.
Now your tomatoes ripen too quickly,
harvest of fruit and scent of mulch brewed
in August heat that strains, unsteadies you.
I'd rather you had a cane of polished wood,
gift of the nymph's taut flesh, its youthful sheen

your support, or at least my arm through yours
as we walk beside those ferns that undulate,
a rippling efflorescence of the forest floor,
beneath tall pines that stand beyond your field,
bare, except for needles near the top
that breathe above our path and ache for light.

IN MY DREAM OF EMILY DICKINSON

Set high on a shelf above my reach
by my mother passing through the room
a photograph of you, Emily—
the original daguerreotype
from Mt. Holyoke, your hair drawn back,
ribbon at your neck, eyes steady, direct,
arm resting near a book; no added ruff
or curls that later sold your work.
Near me on the couch, a toddler—peach skin,
unspeaking—sits on a woman's lap,
is bounced on her knee: an odd vision
of maternity, I realize—this "child"
a porcelain doll that doesn't blink or breathe,
its mother carrying on as if it were alive.

What do you think as you gaze down
at the toy's vacant stare swallowing
the room, its perfect flush caught, well-turned,
to suggest what isn't there—lifeblood
of hand and wrist conveyed in paint?
Why not turn to your herbarium instead,
its best specimens plucked from your garden
or the woods, dried, parchment-bound, Latin names
scored in your precise script? You're the child
of your father's house, your step soft

as a bird that frightens easily,
ruffles its nerves to rhyme's flight, retreats
to a single room with *saturated Sight*
to meet apart *With just the Door ajar,*

and I in the hall, thinking to come in.
What would I find? Your devoted care
of your own sweet mother, affectionate
but ill; your father's stern preoccupations?
Your life is *Like a Cup*—you say—*Discarded*
of the Housewife; the doll, bisque skin cracked,
nests in the dark. You bow-tie your words
into fascicles you tuck in drawers,
while wind rattles the spring garden,
tumbles blossoms' heads, splattered paths
petal-drenched, your mind's heat
staining each page, the storm's quiet eye.
I'm on the threshold, Emily, salvation or despair,
your room washed in that white light—

II. GRACE

MORNING IN THE PUBLIC GARDEN

Unrecognizable,
after trenchant cold,
these flower beds filled
with buds and leaves
while trees still brood
over footpaths smeared
with useless sand
grating underfoot
now the ice is gone.

Who planted all these—
that couldn't have sprung
from last year's bulbs—
appearing in a day?

Predictable, of course,
this green bursting,
the rows of hyacinths
I should have bent low
to breathe, but passed by.

I imagine an armful,
cut stems exposed,
shriveling to the touch
of warming breeze,
and my arms bolstering
their heavy heads.

CHRISTINE CASSON

I'd place them
in the hands
of that woman curled
in blankets near the path
her fingers gripping
in sleep her empty cup—

each petal streaked
with letters of lament,
pale as the boy
Apollo loved,
his neck snapped
by a discus
the god hurled,
as if a god's play
mattered in the world,
or a flower given
in useless sympathy.

No. Better not inhale
such intense perfume,
the gods' transformation
an open wound.
                    Leave it
splayed—just there.

WEIGH MY LIGHT WINGS

She tripped, slammed both knees, hard
against cement. Curled in pain,
body drenched in sweat, she rocked
herself to calm, tried to stand
without success, bones shattered.
After, she limped; past seventy,
would struggle home with groceries,
the pain severe when she stood
        or walked too long.

She wondered that her attention
turned from the path, a moment's
distraction—billowed sky, wing-
glint of birds, the jostled tree.
She'd reached for, without thought,
that leaf bud fuller than the rest,
sepals flared, bursting; stumbled,
the ground surging, swelling against
        her palms outstretched—

as though it were desire, a garden
drowsed with warmth, that woman,
unsuspecting, young, who'd grasped
with casual hand an apple,

smoothest, rose-red, dangling
from the tree and for the taking;
who like her, forgot vigilance,
that stern voice, and time: the sword
that bars return.

THE BEACH AT HULL

A concrete wall and metal fence divide
macadam and wet sand, strewn with kelp
from the morning's tide. By noon, the Atlantic,
limp, laps the shore. Across the street, a diner,
blue-green and mirrored silver to remind us
of the sea, steams clams "every afternoon."
Ours are full of sand; grainy puddles blotch
our roughened plates. Jeannie owns it, locals say,
comes from the "alphabet neighborhood,"—small
clapboard homes set on crowded lots—lives on "Y,"
has been serving food for more than forty years.

Here, mid-day, mid-week, retirees gather
to lessen their time alone, talk of family,
children grown, the friends that would have joined them,
maneuver walkers through the chairs' tight maze,
park them like shopping carts beside the walls.
A glass of chardonnay or beer, white fish
on pulpy bread with chips, and slaw chopped fine
that's easy to digest—they pass the afternoon,
while we watch pigeons waddle by, seagulls peck
halfheartedly at weeds, the ocean's murky swell
out-turned, buttressing the iron clamp of sky.

CHRISTINE CASSON

THEY

sit three or four together at odd angles
to each other, facing helter-skelter,

here on a garden glove matted with earth,
or on a rotting shelf of half-filled paint cans

deep in the garage (others sit alone)
until, struck suddenly by what isn't done,

two (or three) rush off to inspect a bicycle—
its spokes and seat bright pink, and the tassels,

dangling prettily from the handlebars,
soft lipstick shades of orchid and mauve—

landing for a moment, then lifting off,
considering size and style, the quality

of axles and gears at close range. Enough
time spent, one heads away, full tilt, to settle

on the rim of a clay pot, his arrival inciting
those already present to launch off, like

rockets trying to break gravity's hold,
a wild, unruly dance of intensity

and indirection, a mercurial pattern,
that will slow to a hypnotic steady thrum.

An awkward dart, buzz—then nose-diving
to a halt, the same pot, to rifle through

a few inches of old soil, or look on
with humming admonition and advice.

Across the floor, more of them swarm noisily
toward a large bag of earthworm castings

attracted by its rich scent over-ripened
in humid air (better than manure),

are joined by others, more and more, an ever-
swelling crowd, milling, enlarging, contracting,

textured, rippling passivities of air,
endlessly assembling, reassembling themselves.

CHRISTINE CASSON

The next day: utter quiet, they've left no sign,
their important work done, or incomplete,

as though they'd never been. The pot rests coolly
in the dim light, the cans, the bag, the bike

all wait expectantly for who comes next,
stirs up the dust, then leaves without a trace.

CAMEOS

This mummy's flesh is stretched tightly over bone,
cascading hair tangled over knife-edged bone.

I've been to the butcher; he cut me fresh meat.
I cooked it so tender it fell from the bone.

The face of our neighbor's child glows like dull plastic.
"She takes after me," he boasts—no trace of bone.

A dog sniffs our bushes, then shits on our lawn.
Dogs can deceive—I thought he'd dig for a bone.

When a softball slammed the pitcher's chiseled face,
his jaw splintered like china, to bits of bone.

Model homes are painted a neutral color
"that anyone will like"—the color of bone.

You've been ill so long you'd rather stay in bed.
Beneath your milk-blue skin there's too much bone.

Clumps of brackish snow float jauntily in slush.
Is this what it means to be "chilled to the bone?"

Christine totters down the walk over slick ice,
her skin wrapped tight and warm. Underneath is bone.

CHRISTINE CASSON

THE PORTION

You offer me dessert, cake *al morte,*
and I eat, hungrily.
Persian violets on my dresser expand
and reach—
they breathe as they grow.
I lie beside my mother
as insects gather, a murmuring swarm,
into my mouth and ears.

SLIP KNOT

I.

I sat at my father's feet as he wrapped the twine
around his index finger, pulled it taut into a single
knot, then cinched it again, before I could read
its course, that second knot different from the first, nestled
by its side, anchor to a loop that would slide with ease
to any size I liked. If he'd been well his eyes, pleased,
would have gleamed, for a moment, at my confusion—
before his easy *Look closely, I'll show you again.*

Now, it was an effort to perform this usual task,
eyes hard pressed to turn down, to focus on his hands
though his fingers like a potter's recalled the routine,
so he hardly had to look. He would do it once more,
satisfy my compulsion to preserve this simple skill
that would be lost like so much else when he was gone
though it tired him, all motion deliberate, limbs weighted
with his illness, a slow transformation into stone.

CHRISTINE CASSON

II.

The slip knot isn't sound
as its name suggests,
must be used with care
to raise floating objects
fallen overboard, their heft
tightening the knot's grip
easily released,
though in our house
it appeared regularly,
its noose sliding, expanding
or contracting to fit,
pulled close to secure.
My mother, forced to move
when my father died
never fully unpacked:
What use have I for these?—
I don't entertain—
would open over time
incidental packages
still sealed with tape,
the vases and bowls
wadded with newspaper,
linens folded in tissue

thin with wear.
Hesitant to part
with her rich cargo,
she'd set them on the floor:
I'd like you to have this . . .
and this . . . when I die—
but make for me, would you?—
a few lengths of cord
to keep these boxes
closed while you're away.
And I turn to the work
at hand, unravel line
into usable lengths,
spin loops
that will suffice, for now,
against the slip of earth,
its silent undertow.

CHRISTINE CASSON

TO MELVILLE, NEAR DEATH

after reading your letters to Hawthorne

In your fluid script, the image painted
    is of a young man overcome by passion
for an elder writer unacquainted
    with the impulsiveness of youth, its fashion
for overstatement, admiration rolling
    from your pen, your soul stirred as when one gazes
at another, finds oneself, and no controlling
    that blast of recognition that amazes.

Like Ahab, the portrait you created
    overwhelmed; you hadn't foreseen, doting
on each word, you'd be refused, defeated,
    your *eager agitation* brought to nothing,
intentions snuffed by circumstance's pleasure:
    The sailor's tattooed skin?—unrealized treasure.

WE ALL KNOCK

    ~after Zbigniew Herbert's "A Knocker"~

You would strike a board
knock - knock
with thud of gaveled fist
until it answers—

a dry clucking,
no - no
like the clicking of brown sticks—
the imagination stripped,
austere as stone,

and would insist
that this is clarity—
where the river turns
to mud and brittle vegetation,
where dogs sniff;

have us think that beauty
is an easy stream that springs
from the head
effortlessly,
gurgling like a child,
sun-garnished
under a blue bell of sky;

CHRISTINE CASSON

not this *rapping, rapping,*
rapping that I do,
of wood
back to a trunk's concentric rings,
roots kneading into earth,
muscling into soil, until
it will sustain
that bell of green,
that spread of sky;
yes — yes

APOPHATIC

It's quiet—so quiet—these few hours
snatched near the close of an afternoon—

no screeching children, no cars, no birds,
no conversation, everything settled

into itself, the earth holding its breath,
as though it ceased turning; neither heavy clouds

nor sun, but steady light, dull glow of gray,
no rain, no certain wind, an untranslated

pause, this exhale of curtains a shallow
breathing that won't last. My body listens hard,

drinks of this rich calm, almost too fragile
to hold, or hear, this fullness that floods all,

my senses flushed with this potent drug
that whispers in my ear, a haunting voice

that wears away—my hunger to be sated
only when I lie down late, in dark, alone.

CHRISTINE CASSON

NO COLD HEAVEN

No cold heaven, though many houses
on this block need paint and care: lopsided
porch stairs, windows filmed with soot, facades
an accidental patchwork of repair—
cracked wood, sullen brick and stone.

I turned away last night when two men fought,
clawed one another in numbing cold,
palms swathed in rags, a ferocious dance
punctuated by their ear-thrumming roars,
the soiled blankets and layers of clothing
they wore in their way as they wrestled
for a smidgeon of steamy warmth—
the single manhole's pluming breath.

These days of heavy gray and ice propel
all forward toward year's end, blackened snow
blanketing what it can—these littered,
greasy streets—and my misgivings hushed
in well-lit rooms, or the circle of this single lamp.

Today, in the bargain shop nearest the store
where checks are cashed, fiber optic angels,
in nylon taffeta robes of pink and peach

grasp hard their 'candle' bulbs. Pastel lights
play around their wings that rise and fall
stirring the plangent air—otherworldly
whispers like undulations of lost birds.
They hold, sweet, their pale plastic stares.

FUCHSIA

Each bud sprung—dancers
        in pirouette, satin
    dresses spinning, spun
in bursts of wind—the fuchsia
        is in bloom,
    the same plant that hung
last summer by a thread,
        one that she,
    unable to discard
alive, watered, fed,
        coaxed to health,
    bringing it indoors,
then out, a long year's work,
        as though it were a child.
    She felt, she thought,
the neighbors smirk
        when she tended
    its straggly stem,
her labors spent on a stick—
        Why does she waste
    her time? Better
if she found a part-time job, changed
        the baby's diapers,
    cleaned the house or yard.

Now they wonder at the ballet
            unfolding on her porch:
    preening roses, swaying
bergamot, and center stage,
            like gypsy arabesques,
    these flowers' skirted flight.

CHRISTINE CASSON

GRACE

Gnats swarm in the red shaft of lowering
sun, a chaos of dives, swirls towering
as we circumvent the frenzied cloud
to the patio, settle in a garden chair
just out of their way, wrought-iron flowers
at our backs. This dance of confusion
could have sprung from the fuss of a human day,
the endless ring of cell phones, car alarms,
avalanche of emails with *something* to say,
a gaggle of information from circling
memos, voicemail, the TV's non-stop prattle.

Our bergamot launches high and purple
in deepening air, its rich stain refashioned
in shadows that pool the cooling ground,
and one last bee hums hungrily around petals
spiked wide by steady heat, an alluring runway
to the pollinated core, sticky sweet,
drenched in secret scent. The seduction
is hesitant at first, a taste, another sip,
a meditative hovering, and then the diving in.
The flower's head bows ever so slightly,
a tremor runs the length of its stiff stem.

On the patio we sit and talk (the day
still well-lit near its end) of daily things: work, home,
my mother growing old—where will she live?—
the meal we'll prepare together. We savor
our wine to the gnats' buzz, the quieting street,
the turning in, rise and fall of our murmured speech
like those million small black flecks lifting—a sail
lightly stirred by air. We hadn't seen before
how they shift, spin awry, away, and then reverse,
a fluid thrumming cell drawn back to the pattern
of a beat that sways and sings beyond our measure.

CHRISTINE CASSON

III. As If Of Wings

~Fanny Mendelssohn-Hensel, 1805-1847~

Von den Bergen zu den Hügeln
Niederab das Tal entlang,
Da erklingt es wie von Flügeln . . .
—Johann Wolfgang von Goethe

And the bird called, in response to
The unheard music hidden in the shrubbery . . .
—T. S. Eliot

PRELUDE

Through window glass the garden
rests and waits, or comes to itself,
a cyclic recognition of air and light,
distance, degree of sun,
absence or excess of rain, visitations
of insects, birds, the temperature of life
to nurture or thwart unpredictable

as the wavering lens of these panes,
sand-and lime-fused, potash-cooled,
their seeds and reams hovering, rippling
the earth, quickening the trunks of trees.

From behind this flickering membrane
that holds the blower's breath
the landscape sets about its living business—
the curve of vine and leaf brushed
by day or night, buds flowering,
fragrance and petal-touch,
straining to completion or giving up,
and in either case, the absent aftermath, all
as it should be, after all . . .

THE TEACHER

Marie Bigot was dead at thirty-four.
The women who knew her recounted her life—
how she wouldn't pay attention to her health
but, obstinate, would teach and perform
despite her frailty; would overuse her gifts—
enough to hasten any woman's death.

Reportedly, when Haydn heard her play
he could almost believe she'd composed
his music herself, his strains become hers—
so closely she'd repeat what he had meant—
but transformed, her fingers pressuring keys
to speak a tongue now strange, no longer his.

And Beethoven, hearing her interpret
his "Appassionata"—how she plumbed
his human depths with sweet, dark notes,
the sonata's taut form intensified
by her command of the new six-octave
Hammerclavier—gave Bigot his manuscript.

When she removed it from its case of inlaid
wood, untied its ribbon for her best student
to see, the pages unscrolled to hushed air,

the scrawled notes impressed into parchment
by so fervent a hand Fanny stood transfixed,
the scribbled ink like needles stitching sound

though no one played, conveying an intensity
the young girl longed to hear, to understand.
Marie would guide her swiftness on the keys,
whose parents had her study with the best
in Paris, would encourage her to play,
this child with *Bach'sche Fugenfinger*,

a nimble strength she worked hard to achieve,
exercises for her fourth and fifth fingers
repeated daily until she could summon
Bach's *Well-Tempered Clavier* from memory,
the church organist's preludes and fugues crowding
the quiet room, a counterpoint of song.

Still, her aunts would lament in loud whispers
that she was least pretty and too precocious,
unlikely to attend to those small details
a woman should—as they paced, gracefully,
those hushed parlors, patted their hair, feathers
rustling, brushing against their lustrous cage.

DEAR FELIX

~Fanny Mendelssohn-Hensel~

You're sorely missed by all of us:
            when the staircase door opens
at teatime, we call out together
            "Felix has come," though of course
we know you must stay on, prolong
            this necessary trip, let Goethe,
the master, consider your talent,
            whether it should be encouraged.

Since you've gone I've fallen ill,
            can't manage the piano, or sing,
a cough so harsh mother cringes
            at the sound, an aggressive guest
that leaves me spent in mind and limb
            like our garden elm, its leaves like notes
prematurely turned, drifting
            where we sat before you left.

You must tell me everything
            Goethe says—remember every word!—
and sketch his house to copy
            in my book, memorize each room,

every moment gathering to form
        your years ahead: the instrument
he keeps, the keys' response, the scores
        performed that meet with most success.

My own composition sheets, unmarked,
        refract the mid-day glare; the bare
staves in formation, their latent
        songs, seem to balk at my touch;
thoughts like a girdled chrysalis,
        wax-wrapped, untransformed,
hindered as my shoulders in this
        woolen shawl I wear for warmth.

Your lessons received from Hummel
        you must convey when you return—
tone color, harmonics, the gift
        we shared. Here, we talk of Goethe,
his eminence all the stir, who'll be
        father to you if you impress,
are chosen, good brother, my student
        become my eyesight and my hands.

PROGRAMME MUSIC

Was it lightheadedness, a stomach-flutter
you felt when you read your father's letter
written from Paris, his response to your lieder?

Never mind the flurry of inspiration,
weeks when you could hardly separate pen
from paper, the years of preparation

realized in those new compositions,
and, after, your elation with everything—
the garden, conversation, your ink-stained hands.

He spoke of your forthcoming confirmation,
a Christian path chosen for his daughter
who must *devote her soul, her intelligence*

to motherhood, home, the highest improvements
for a young woman of your accomplishments
for whom *music must remain an ornament.*

Did you wonder, then, at your education—
a young prodigy's rigorous training,
your father's attentiveness to your playing?

You were "as gifted" as your brother,
his confidante and musical advisor
possessed of a talent surpassing his.

How quickly were you able to smother
your stricken stare, left at home to embroider?
Felix would travel to see the great Goethe,

wander Paris like a country of desire,
while you turned graciously towards marriage,
though Hensel saw what thrummed behind your eyes.

What remedy, what prospects could he propose
now that you'd slipped—diminuendo—
behind a curtain, into shadow?

INTERLUDE

To enter life as summer—
       roots set deep, nourished in soil
fragrant with heat,
   flowers drawn open by sun:

the corolla of a rose, each petal
       peeling back from its potent core;
clematis's swan neck
   stretched tight, sepals splayed:

deep purple pools punctuating sky,
       a profusion of semitones
chorus to the day's full blue,
   easeful, become what they will:

like fingers rippling the piano's keys,
       or steadying the violin's strings
to certain pitch, transforming sound
   even as they are transformed:

minding, knowing what's to come—
       ardent afternoon, evening's stain,
hypnotic counterpoint of steady rain,
   the light—pregnant, long.

ZAUBERMANTEL

Hard to believe they had just come from a walk,
their path taking them through forests of beech trees,
past the crumbling walls of the Cistercian abbey,
vines curled around ruins like meandering songs.

The soft silence of aged mortar and stone
brushed the ear, the strange geometric
of broken arch and gable cleaving,
petitioning the air: *So God created*

humankind in his image . . . Male and female
he created them . . . placed them in a garden.
And when they reached the town, the painted sills
and masonry facades so like the factory

their grandfather owned—its floor of dye-baths,
looms, skeins of yarn, the world he wove to veil
his crooked frame—seemed to watch them pass.
The words pierced their ears like dull needles

tearing cloth: *Judenjungen! Judenjungen!*
The young children wandering the streets
of Dobberan followed Felix and Fanny
for blocks. Lost siblings in a fairy tale,

their hastened pace matched by their pursuers,
Felix's head throbbed when he abruptly turned,
fended taunting shoves with fists and yells.
They never thought to hide themselves, to slip

inside their family's *Zaubermantel*—
magic cloak to hide their Jewish blood, its silk
so finely drafted, spun, it could keep them safe,
or make them disappear in a wisp of smoke.

THE PORTRAIT

She's turned her head
to gaze over her shoulder
at something unseen by the viewer;
in a graceful portrait-pose,
intelligent eyes, straight nose
like her mother's,
full lips, handsomely curved—

those reports of her ugliness
unfounded, not here, not in this portrait
by her husband-to-be,
one arm draped in robes,
the other smooth and white,
and her hair elegantly drawn
into a wreath—flushed flowers,
buds like bunched grapes
falling to her neck.

When the likeness was completed,
she found it strange—too pretty—
hard to see herself that way:
her sternness softened, her hunched back
hidden from sight,

CHRISTINE CASSON

that "contraption" of petals,
and all those ardent waves
framing her face.

Didn't he notice she wore
her center-parted hair
tightly gathered,
flat against her face, moonlike,
only interrupted
by her eyebrows' thick wings?
What would her family think?

And Felix was quick to object,
who had become her eyes and ears,
his letters full of travel and his work
while she remained at home.
He'd known his sister longer:
her spirit was not the rapture of flowers,
but an inner rapture, to be discovered gradually.
And she agreed.

She couldn't see the beauty Hensel saw,
his portrait a lacework of harmonies
like light beyond her vision's field—
everything she'd wish herself to be.

CRADLESONG

~Fanny Mendelssohn-Hensel~

A miracle to birth a child—Sebastian
looks at me with sweet eyes, his new world

my own, his care my complete absorption,
a composition that breathes fullest music,

this passage I accepted, this door
I unexpectedly opened, fulfilling, filled.

How soon these hours will pass, these first
months an exclusive gift, his small hands, feet,

perfect limbs growing, grown, become memory,
like so much else, my own childhood, the music

I shared with Felix, the years' busy silences
stretched between us like unwritten songs,

the faint impress of our intermittent letters
and few days together a plaintive fading note

like those unfinished manuscripts I've tucked
in a drawer, dimming glimmers of melody.

CHRISTINE CASSON

Again the world turns towards turbulence:
a Russian frigate anchors in the harbor

at Swinemünde, its cannons polished
to a fervent sheen, its armory a box

of cradled jewels tended like the rarest
works of art, carefully wrought to destroy.

How will we be judged by some future race
wiser than we, who will devise a peace;

what will they see when they look back—
an unfolding symphony, or a crumpled page?

INTERLUDE

Flowers fold, fall,
dispersed in wind
but for a few
that bloom despite
desiccative light,
the corn's silk
chastened,
furred lamb's ear
weathered in sun—
a lingering heat
pursing pear, grape,
each seed bursting
like a burgeoning
composition, notes
selected, seasoned
with time to tumble
from the page,
into restive space
or slip by unheard—
and afterwards,
flagging leaves,
their sheen brushed
dull in increments,
leathery like skin
grown wizened,
its creases deepening.

CHRISTINE CASSON

SONNTAGSMUSIK

–Fanny Mendelssohn-Hensel–

Yesterday, one hundred guests filled this room,
waiting for my concert to begin,
frescoed ceiling and tapestry walls
lit by June sun, glass doors swung open
to roses in bloom, full-leafed vines
spiraling pillars, embowering the portico.

I've launched the tragic *Iphigenie,*
my soloists' three voices interweaving,
heightening each other as I've never heard before:
Mantius and Bader unsurpassed in their duet,
and Decker fierce in her sacrificial role
of Agamemnon's daughter brilliantly betrayed.

My Sunday child thrives, draws an ever larger
more distinguished crowd—the best musicians,
my choir in full voice. At last, I have a free hand.
Then comes again this quiet room. I sit,
piano closed, all traces gone but spent bouquets
and some few lingering harmonies and tones.

THE MISCARRIAGE

~Fanny Mendelssohn-Hensel~

I've lost my second child.
It slid from me the way those sheets of ice
rush from our roof on winter afternoons,
almost silent as they plunge to lingering snow,
their transparency lost in that white surround,
   as though they never were.

  When my stomach swelled,
throbbed with quickening life, I thought
that vital energy might break my long
interval of silence, who couldn't write
for years, wrestling with notes, yet with such ease
   could conceive a child.

  I've cared for husband, son,
fulfilled my social duties as required,
plagued all the while with headaches of my own,
a part of me dismissed, alone, slipped inside a draw,
to someday be withdrawn—a curiosity
   from years before.

  CHRISTINE CASSON

What part of me is this,
gone, asleep, a space that's been closed off,
a gate rusted shut—my music not performed,
unknown, my strength insufficient to sustain
this child that won't be born but dissipates, part-formed
        unable to endure?

    Since then I've felt weighted,
heavy as the peonies that droop beside
my garden's edge, each calyx gorged, pushed
to bursting, petal upon petal rushing forth,
stems unable to raise each encephalitic head
        from graveled path to sun.

FROM THE GARDEN

~Lea Mendelssohn~

Snow covers these slender stems where several months before
   one last late rosebud bloomed, each petal tightly creased
around the next like carefully chosen notes, like pointed words
   I wrote to Felix, begging him to encourage you
             to publish your work.
Frilled in white gauze, they bend, now, in the winter blast,
   malleable as your long, slim hands, gracing the keys'
             expanse of white and black.

Here, apart from husband, children, the management
   of home, I can think; a haven even in this cold,
away from neighbors' eyes, their taut cheeks, the stiff
   slight-smile of greeting when we meet, the empty stare
            that masks their disregard
for Jews, *so swarthy, odd—how different they are. How*
   do they live at home? We comport ourselves like dolls
            under their scrutiny.

Your father understood the need for appearances,
   urged you, Fanny, to consider your brother's career,
to "act as a woman should," your own music steeped
   in shadow like violets that hug the ground each year
            in our trees' summer shade;

CHRISTINE CASSON

would have his family near invisible, as well-disguised
    as this garden's contours obscured now by fallen lace,
            a more graceful leveler.

From this path I see your concert room through leaded glass,
    the piano wavering as if alive, as it is when you play,
the ceiling's high cupola refracting sound washing
    through the room like mounting showers that cleanse,
            and silence following.
You've lost yourself, daughter, afraid your life's been cropped.
    Write, amend your meager space, transpose this chill soil
            into your signature, flourishing.

COUNTERPOINT

~Fanny Mendelssohn-Hensel and Felix Mendelssohn~

I had to wait until Felix was old enough
for our lessons to begin.

I was impatient, but he was clever —
we learned almost as one.

How I hungered for instruction, to prod
those notes I heard inside my head,

to write them out on staves
so I could hear aloud

what I longed to say. Music
enveloped hours that paused

and passed, without my knowing,
undistracted by those trinkets,

attentions other girls sought,
or by appearances—

my pronounced nose, stooped back,
and eyebrows, black as my father's.

The melodies we fashioned
opened amplitudes —

CHRISTINE CASSON

chords, progressions, harmonics —
the pale walls, coffered ceilings

infused with sound,
register of change,

like an aroma of tea leaves
that modulates in air.

*****

I've fathered my first child, a son,
and for three years have directed

Leipzig's Gewandhaus Orchestra
yet still I won't enter competitions.

I recall, when I was young, contests
with Fanny, my few chords wheedled

into noise, her melodies wound like vines
around the carved tables, chairs scattered

in our practice room, and imagine
my rivals, eager to test their strength,

concentrations of will that explode:
—I cannot muster a note.

Older, my "Cantor," she understood
my compositions, her ear my own.

Even now, after years of success
I send her manuscripts, solicit

her advice. Of course, she won't publish
without my approval, and shouldn't.

Being well brought up to tend to home
as father wished, how could she sustain

an oeuvre, a progression of work,
and publishing a serious matter?

Still I almost hear them—dissonant strains
that sear, sweep beyond resolution....

CHRISTINE CASSON

INTERLUDE

Winter clamps hard
    around hydrangea trunk,
broken lavender stem,
    ivy crisped with cold,
as if run through flame,
    crumbling when touched,
disintegrating, ash-flakes
    flown in the beige-gray
of grass and fallow light.

Unused, the garden room—
    a blank stave; piano shut,
bench tucked beneath,
    no manuscripts strewn
over tabletops or chaise,
    no opening doors
or mirrored glance, flash
    of hand or voice
to arrest the marble chill.

No reason now to stare
    through the window's
furrowed pane, remnant
    of the blower's gasping

breath, its quivering a lie
   when all lies so still,
the garden's iron will
   turning the eye away, sod
sealed tight as stone.

CHRISTINE CASSON

TO THE SOUTH

The journey to Italy began in your youth
    among vaulted cliffs of the Saint Gotthard Pass,
its rock-scrabbled trail through thundering Reuss gorge
    in the Swiss Alps softening to flowering
meadow-valleys and the green hills of Andermatt,
    glaciered mountains just beyond so proximate
        to Italian soil it recast the natives' speech.

In a letter to your cousin you imagined,
    if a man, you'd have traveled alone
those final miles to the border, freed from constraint
    or concern for who'd accompany you,
to where *the plain adorns itself*—corn grass, aloe,
    olive tree and cypress, one fair, one dark—poised
        in blue air, and sun poured like wine across the fields.

You'd wait seventeen years, Felix's letters
    quickening with the promise: to arrive in Rome,
city of ruins, art remaking each fissure;
    city of sacred music, masses and plainchant
echoing towards you as you strained to draw near
    the wrought iron grill of the Sistine Chapel,
        its ceiling, walls, lush with color and sound.

When Carnival arrived you surprised yourself,
    took to the streets with munitions of sweetmeats,
flowers to throw at the revelers that climbed
    the running board of your coach, elegant masks
muting their lighthearted words, costumes like paint
    spattering the path of the Corso, fantasies
        and farces play-acted to bedlam and noise—

so unlike the Villa Medici's serene façade,
    its precise ornamentation home
to the Académie de France, where Gounod
    and Bousquet listened raptly to your Bach,
sought your knowledge of German composition,
    your talents so admired in those hushed rooms
        that you, in excitement, couldn't stop composing.

An incomparable musician and pianist
    Gounod later wrote, *her intelligence revealed*
in deep eyes and a fiery gaze, his words
    marking open your path like a milestone,
your confidence unsheathed like those insouciant
    blooms softening the stiff geometry
        of the Medici gardens' array of hedge

CHRISTINE CASSON

and statuary, groves where you rehearsed
    musicians in the rich afternoon sun
for intimate evening concerts—lights in town,
    fireflies, a church illuminating soft air—
or wrote, the melodies, harmonic progressions,
    forming to words with precision and ease,
      of the south . . . land of eternal blossom.

SONG

~Felix Mendelssohn~

When I asked Queen Victoria to sing
            a song of her choice
from my volume of lieder
                she chose three
of my sister's,
            Fanny's rich melodies
                most gratifying.

To admit they weren't mine was hard
            even after years
of success composing,
                my first collection
strung through with Fanny's work,
            the only way her compositions
                could be heard—

commonplace for a man to publish
            under his own name
a woman's score who wouldn't
                on her own,
notes threaded to tendrils of sound,
            her harmonic language
                exquisite.

I felt my face flush, taken by surprise,
        accustomed to calling
them mine, this discomfiture
            as though I'd done wrong,
unwelcome agitation,
        a lingering melody that flickers
            and moves on.

INTERLUDE

What soft stirrings fool the ear?

When frost-fretted earth needles with cold,
ice-clinched gusts crusting grass, the sod
hard, inward-turned,

look to soil, call dead nettle to appear,
tender leaf-ears heart-shaped, rims
deeply stained.

Whispering vegetation will creep to motion,
sap seep through veins clenched
straining

like a mind's route through shards of sound,
the blank stave wheedled into song,
notes wrested

the way the pupa, wings paper-thin, lifts
past its own encasement
into air—

so this frantic surge— : A pallid leaflet
unfurls, breathes—
and—greener—is.

A GARDEN OPUS

In emergent spring her garden flourishes,
            tumbles forth: tulips stumble
over crocuses, sweet william creeps, reaching
            into violet beds, almond tree
and apricot pour down blossoms,
                        a carpet of pastels.

Outside her walled haven the rustling
            of politics, upheaval, pamphlets
spouting socialist ideals, protesting
            the authoritarian state,
the *Landtag* formed—like an agitated breeze
                        that circles, stops,

starts: unsettled intentions. Fanny, restless,
            delighted with the early warmth,
the steady visits of musicians, composes—
            a grand trio, song after song—
can only recall such happiness in Rome,
                        and as a young child.

Now this windfall of offers to publish,
            and colleagues' urging
in spite of Felix's cold displeasure.

Her eagerness brims, infectious,
like whorls of unpruned honeysuckle,
                        sweet pea burgeoning

with each printed page: a world unfolds,
                        her own and strange, tumultuous
flowering she thought too late; dormant
                        perennial drawn upward, awakening—
You are repose, and gentle peace; you are longing,
                        and longing's reward.

CHRISTINE CASSON

LIEBESLIED

~Wilhelm Hensel~

They've lowered you
into the earth, love,
the first born first
to depart, your hands
folded in repose
as you'd rest them
in your lap when
society called, your art
set aside, long fingers
that would flare across
the keys, weave
your polyphonies—
expanded, opposed,
reestablished—all
you'd taught my
untrained ear.

Your death is
our Sunday concert,
your coffin covered
with flowers
in the Gartenhaus—
its brilliant light,

unbroken panorama
of paths and trees—
all of us stunned
by how suddenly
your playing
stopped, fingers
stricken, notes
damper-locked,
fallen inward,
unpetalling . . .

I paint your portrait
to fill the silence,
your eyes steady,
burnished
as though the sun
had taken root—
what I'd always
imagined, your
happiness revealed
in your final lied—
Clouds draw down,
the bird soon settles . . .
what rapture to gaze
high above the blue
deep clearness
of the sky's dome.

Coda: Arrangement

~i.m. Lawrence V. Casson, 1923-1998~

When I was young and heard
        the vinyl record drop, and music lift
                from the lumbering Magnavox

weekend afternoons, watched the needle
        thrum its course through spiraled grooves,
                and you, father,

in your chair, arms relaxed, reclining
        on its rests or folded in your lap
                after the long week's work,

I didn't know it was a gift—
        chords and notes enwound
                in evanescing strands

while you inclined your face
        absorbed in shimmered sound,
                your fingers sometimes moving

in the living room's soft air
        as over keys you couldn't play
                like wings of nesting birds.

Christine Casson

Fanny Mendelssohn Hensel (1805-1847), pianist and composer, wrote at a time when it was considered unsuitable for a woman from the upper classes to have ambitions as a professional musician. She composed numerous piano pieces, songs, duets, trios, a capella choral works, cantatas, chamber music, an overture, and an oratorio. However, as sister to the composer Felix Mendelssohn she was, both during her life and afterwards, overshadowed by her brother, remembered more for her letters and diaries in relation to him than for her own compositions, or for her brilliance as a player and conductor in drawing rooms and salons. Though the bond between Fanny and Felix was close from an early age, upon reaching adolescence, their paths diverged—he to become a professional musician and she to marry the court painter Wilhelm Hensel, who encouraged her talents. Though her Sonntags-musiken were prestigious musical events in Berlin, Felix discouraged publication of her compositions as their father also had done before he died. It was only a year before her death that she broke free of her brother's influence and began to publish, meeting with immediate success. At the height of her creativity, she suffered a fatal stroke during a rehearsal for one of her Sunday concerts.

The epigraph is from "Wanderlied ("Wanderer's Song") by Johann Wolfgang von Goethe, set to music by Fanny Mendelssohn-Hensel:

> *From the mountains to the hills,*
> *Resounding through the valleys,*
> *There's music, as if of wings . . .*

trans. Bettina Reinke-Welsh

Author photograph by Star Black

CHRISTINE CASSON'S poems have been published in *Agenda, Dalhousie Review, Natural Bridge, Stand, Slant, South Dakota Review,* and *Alabama Literary Review,* and in the anthologies *Fashioned Pleasures* (Parallel Press, 2005), *Never Before* (Four Way Books, 2005), and *Conversation Pieces* (Everyman's, 2007). She has also published essays on the work of Leslie Marmon Silko and the poetry of Linda Hogan, as well as non-fiction. She earned her MFA from the Program for Writers at Warren Wilson College, and is Scholar/Writer in Residence at Emerson College in Boston.

Printed in the USA
CPSIA information can be obtained
at www.ICGtesting.com
LVHW091159141024
793748LV00001B/63